50 Recipes Passed Down With Love

By: Kelly Johnson

Table of Contents

- Grandma's Classic Meatloaf
- Mom's Homemade Chicken Pot Pie
- Great-Aunt's Sweet Potato Casserole
- Family-Style Spaghetti Bolognese
- Grandma's Old-Fashioned Mac and Cheese
- Dad's Signature Beef Stew
- Nana's Apple Pie
- Family-Style Roasted Chicken
- Great-Grandmother's Lemon Pound Cake
- Mom's Famous Meatballs
- Aunt Clara's Chocolate Chip Cookies
- Grandma's Buttermilk Biscuits
- Family Chili Recipe
- Nana's Cranberry Sauce
- Great-Aunt Helen's Cornbread
- Mom's Banana Bread
- Grandma's Cabbage Rolls

- Aunt June's Potato Salad
- Dad's Barbecue Ribs
- Mom's Chicken and Dumplings
- Great-Grandmother's Frittata
- Grandma's Cinnamon Rolls
- Family Roast Beef with Gravy
- Aunt Millie's Creamy Coleslaw
- Mom's Tomato Soup
- Grandma's Peach Cobbler
- Dad's Fried Chicken
- Nana's Homemade Jam
- Great-Aunt's Stuffing Recipe
- Family Beef Tacos
- Great-Grandmother's Chicken Noodle Soup
- Mom's Stuffed Bell Peppers
- Aunt Mary's Lemon Bars
- Grandma's Shrimp and Grits
- Family-Style Lasagna
- Dad's Clam Chowder

- Grandma's Rhubarb Pie

- Aunt Betty's Pecan Pie

- Mom's Baked Ziti

- Great-Grandmother's Goulash

- Nana's Chicken Fried Steak

- Family Meatloaf Sandwiches

- Great-Aunt's Green Bean Casserole

- Mom's Chocolate Pudding Cake

- Grandma's Steamed Pudding

- Dad's Smoked Sausages

- Aunt Diane's Potato Soup

- Nana's Chocolate Fudge

- Great-Grandmother's Rice Pudding

- Mom's Apple Crisp

Grandma's Classic Meatloaf

Ingredients

- 1 lb ground beef
- 1 egg
- 1 small onion, finely chopped
- 1 cup bread crumbs
- 1/2 cup milk
- 1 tbsp Worcestershire sauce
- 1/2 tsp garlic powder
- 1 tsp salt
- 1/2 tsp black pepper
- 1/4 cup ketchup (for topping)

Instructions

1. Preheat oven to 350°F. Grease a loaf pan.
2. In a large bowl, combine ground beef, egg, chopped onion, bread crumbs, milk, Worcestershire sauce, garlic powder, salt, and pepper. Mix until well combined.
3. Transfer mixture to the loaf pan and shape into a loaf.
4. Spread ketchup over the top of the loaf.
5. Bake for 1 hour. Let rest for 10 minutes before slicing and serving.

Mom's Homemade Chicken Pot Pie

Ingredients

- 2 cups cooked chicken, diced
- 1 cup frozen peas and carrots
- 1/3 cup butter
- 1/3 cup flour
- 1 1/2 cups chicken broth
- 1/2 cup milk
- 1 tsp garlic powder
- 1/2 tsp salt
- 1/4 tsp black pepper
- 1 package refrigerated pie crusts (or homemade)

Instructions

1. Preheat oven to 400°F.
2. In a saucepan, melt butter over medium heat. Stir in flour and cook for 1-2 minutes.
3. Gradually add chicken broth and milk, whisking constantly until the mixture thickens.
4. Stir in chicken, peas and carrots, garlic powder, salt, and pepper. Remove from heat.

5. Roll out one pie crust and place it in a 9-inch pie pan. Pour the chicken mixture into the pie crust.

6. Top with the second pie crust, crimping the edges to seal. Cut slits in the top to allow steam to escape.

7. Bake for 30-35 minutes until golden brown. Let cool for 5 minutes before serving.

Great-Aunt's Sweet Potato Casserole

Ingredients

- 4 medium sweet potatoes, peeled and cubed
- 1/2 cup brown sugar
- 1/4 cup butter, melted
- 1/4 cup milk
- 1 tsp vanilla extract
- 1/2 tsp cinnamon
- 1/4 tsp nutmeg
- 1/2 cup mini marshmallows (optional for topping)

Instructions

1. Preheat oven to 350°F. Grease a casserole dish.
2. Boil sweet potatoes in salted water until tender, about 15-20 minutes. Drain and mash.
3. Mix mashed sweet potatoes with brown sugar, melted butter, milk, vanilla, cinnamon, and nutmeg.
4. Transfer the mixture to the casserole dish and top with marshmallows if using.
5. Bake for 25-30 minutes, or until marshmallows are golden brown. Serve warm.

Family-Style Spaghetti Bolognese

Ingredients

- 1 lb ground beef
- 1 small onion, finely chopped
- 2 cloves garlic, minced
- 1 can (28 oz) crushed tomatoes
- 1/4 cup tomato paste
- 1 tsp dried oregano
- 1 tsp dried basil
- 1/2 tsp salt
- 1/4 tsp black pepper
- 1/2 cup red wine (optional)
- 1 lb spaghetti
- Fresh basil or Parmesan cheese for garnish

Instructions

1. In a large skillet, cook ground beef, onion, and garlic over medium heat until browned, about 7-10 minutes.
2. Add crushed tomatoes, tomato paste, oregano, basil, salt, pepper, and red wine (if using). Stir and simmer for 20-30 minutes.
3. Meanwhile, cook spaghetti according to package instructions.

4. Serve the Bolognese sauce over the cooked spaghetti, garnished with fresh basil or Parmesan.

Grandma's Old-Fashioned Mac and Cheese

Ingredients

- 8 oz elbow macaroni
- 2 cups shredded sharp cheddar cheese
- 1/2 cup milk
- 1/4 cup butter
- 2 tbsp flour
- 1/2 tsp mustard powder
- 1/2 tsp salt
- 1/4 tsp black pepper
- 1/4 tsp paprika (optional)

Instructions

1. Preheat oven to 350°F. Grease a 9x9-inch baking dish.
2. Cook macaroni according to package instructions, drain, and set aside.
3. In a saucepan, melt butter over medium heat. Whisk in flour, mustard powder, salt, pepper, and paprika.
4. Gradually add milk, stirring constantly until the mixture thickens. Stir in shredded cheese until melted and smooth.
5. Mix the cooked macaroni with the cheese sauce and transfer to the baking dish.
6. Bake for 20 minutes until bubbly and golden on top. Serve warm.

Dad's Signature Beef Stew

Ingredients

- 2 lbs beef stew meat, cubed
- 3 carrots, peeled and sliced
- 3 potatoes, peeled and cubed
- 1 onion, chopped
- 3 cloves garlic, minced
- 4 cups beef broth
- 1 tsp dried thyme
- 2 bay leaves
- 1 tbsp tomato paste
- Salt and pepper to taste

Instructions

1. Brown beef stew meat in a large pot over medium heat, then remove and set aside.
2. In the same pot, sauté onion and garlic until softened, about 5 minutes.
3. Add tomato paste and cook for another minute, then return beef to the pot.
4. Add beef broth, carrots, potatoes, thyme, bay leaves, salt, and pepper. Bring to a boil, then reduce heat to low.
5. Cover and simmer for 1.5 to 2 hours, or until beef is tender. Serve warm.

Nana's Apple Pie

Ingredients

- 6 cups sliced apples (preferably Granny Smith)
- 1 cup granulated sugar
- 1 tbsp lemon juice
- 1 tsp ground cinnamon
- 1/2 tsp ground nutmeg
- 1 tbsp flour
- 1 tbsp butter, cut into small pieces
- 1 package pie crusts (or homemade)

Instructions

1. Preheat oven to 425°F.
2. In a large bowl, toss apples with sugar, lemon juice, cinnamon, nutmeg, and flour.
3. Roll out one pie crust and place it in a 9-inch pie pan. Fill with the apple mixture and dot with butter.
4. Top with the second pie crust, crimp edges, and cut slits in the top.
5. Bake for 40-45 minutes until the crust is golden. Let cool before serving.

Family-Style Roasted Chicken

Ingredients

- 1 whole chicken (about 4 lbs)
- 2 tbsp olive oil
- 1 lemon, quartered
- 1 onion, quartered
- 4 cloves garlic, smashed
- 1 tsp salt
- 1/2 tsp black pepper
- 1 tsp dried thyme

Instructions

1. Preheat oven to 400°F. Place chicken in a roasting pan.
2. Stuff chicken with lemon, onion, and garlic.
3. Rub chicken with olive oil, salt, pepper, and thyme.
4. Roast for 1.5 hours or until the internal temperature reaches 165°F. Let rest for 10 minutes before carving.

Great-Grandmother's Lemon Pound Cake

Ingredients

- 2 cups all-purpose flour
- 1 1/2 cups granulated sugar
- 1/2 cup unsalted butter, softened
- 4 large eggs
- 1/2 cup milk
- 2 tsp lemon zest
- 1 tsp vanilla extract
- 1/2 tsp baking powder
- 1/4 tsp salt
- 1/4 cup fresh lemon juice

Instructions

1. Preheat oven to 350°F. Grease a 9x5-inch loaf pan.
2. Beat butter and sugar until creamy. Add eggs, one at a time, and mix well.
3. Add lemon zest, vanilla extract, flour, baking powder, salt, and milk. Mix until smooth.
4. Pour batter into the loaf pan and bake for 55-60 minutes. Let cool before serving.

Mom's Famous Meatballs

Ingredients

- 1 lb ground beef
- 1/2 cup bread crumbs
- 1/4 cup grated Parmesan cheese
- 1 egg
- 2 cloves garlic, minced
- 1 tbsp parsley, chopped
- 1/4 tsp salt
- 1/4 tsp black pepper
- 2 cups marinara sauce

Instructions

1. Preheat oven to 375°F. Grease a baking sheet.
2. In a large bowl, combine ground beef, bread crumbs, Parmesan, egg, garlic, parsley, salt, and pepper.
3. Form into meatballs and place on the baking sheet.
4. Bake for 20-25 minutes until browned.
5. Heat marinara sauce in a saucepan and add cooked meatballs. Simmer for 10 minutes before serving.

Aunt Clara's Chocolate Chip Cookies

Ingredients

- 2 1/4 cups all-purpose flour
- 1 tsp baking soda
- 1/2 tsp salt
- 1 cup unsalted butter, softened
- 3/4 cup granulated sugar
- 3/4 cup packed brown sugar
- 1 tsp vanilla extract
- 2 large eggs
- 2 cups semi-sweet chocolate chips

Instructions

1. Preheat oven to 350°F. Grease baking sheets or line with parchment paper.
2. In a medium bowl, whisk together flour, baking soda, and salt.
3. In a large bowl, cream together butter, granulated sugar, brown sugar, and vanilla extract until light and fluffy.
4. Beat in eggs, one at a time.
5. Gradually add the dry ingredients and mix until just combined. Stir in chocolate chips.
6. Drop rounded tablespoons of dough onto the prepared baking sheets.

7. Bake for 10-12 minutes, or until golden brown. Let cool on baking sheets for 2 minutes before transferring to wire racks to cool completely.

Grandma's Buttermilk Biscuits

Ingredients

- 2 cups all-purpose flour
- 1 tbsp baking powder
- 1/2 tsp baking soda
- 1 tsp salt
- 1/2 cup unsalted butter, cold and cubed
- 3/4 cup buttermilk

Instructions

1. Preheat oven to 450°F. Grease a baking sheet.
2. In a large bowl, whisk together flour, baking powder, baking soda, and salt.
3. Cut in the cold butter using a pastry cutter or your fingers until the mixture resembles coarse crumbs.
4. Pour in buttermilk and stir until the dough just comes together.
5. Turn the dough out onto a floured surface and knead gently 5-6 times. Roll the dough to 1-inch thickness and cut into rounds using a biscuit cutter.
6. Place biscuits on the baking sheet and bake for 12-15 minutes, or until golden brown. Serve warm.

Family Chili Recipe

Ingredients

- 1 lb ground beef
- 1 onion, chopped
- 2 cloves garlic, minced
- 1 can (15 oz) kidney beans, drained and rinsed
- 1 can (15 oz) black beans, drained and rinsed
- 1 can (14.5 oz) diced tomatoes
- 1 can (6 oz) tomato paste
- 1 cup beef broth
- 1 tbsp chili powder
- 1 tsp cumin
- 1/2 tsp smoked paprika
- 1/4 tsp cayenne pepper
- Salt and pepper to taste
- Shredded cheese and sour cream for garnish (optional)

Instructions

1. In a large pot, cook ground beef over medium heat until browned. Remove and drain excess fat.

2. Add chopped onion and garlic to the pot and sauté until softened, about 5 minutes.

3. Add the ground beef back to the pot along with beans, diced tomatoes, tomato paste, and beef broth.

4. Stir in chili powder, cumin, smoked paprika, cayenne, salt, and pepper. Bring to a boil, then reduce heat and simmer for 30 minutes, stirring occasionally.

5. Serve with shredded cheese and sour cream if desired.

Nana's Cranberry Sauce

Ingredients

- 12 oz fresh cranberries
- 1 cup water
- 1 cup granulated sugar
- 1/4 tsp ground cinnamon
- 1/4 tsp ground cloves
- 1/4 tsp orange zest (optional)

Instructions

1. In a saucepan, combine cranberries, water, and sugar. Bring to a boil over medium-high heat.
2. Reduce heat to low and simmer for 10-15 minutes, stirring occasionally, until the cranberries burst and the sauce thickens.
3. Stir in cinnamon, cloves, and orange zest, if using.
4. Remove from heat and let cool before serving.

Great-Aunt Helen's Cornbread

Ingredients

- 1 1/4 cups cornmeal
- 3/4 cup all-purpose flour
- 1 tbsp baking powder
- 1/2 tsp salt
- 1/4 cup sugar
- 1 cup milk
- 2 large eggs
- 1/4 cup unsalted butter, melted

Instructions

1. Preheat oven to 425°F. Grease a 9-inch round or square baking dish.
2. In a large bowl, whisk together cornmeal, flour, baking powder, salt, and sugar.
3. In another bowl, combine milk, eggs, and melted butter. Add the wet ingredients to the dry ingredients and stir until just combined.
4. Pour the batter into the prepared baking dish and bake for 20-25 minutes, or until golden brown and a toothpick inserted comes out clean.
5. Let cool for a few minutes before slicing and serving.

Mom's Banana Bread

Ingredients

- 2-3 ripe bananas, mashed
- 1/3 cup melted butter
- 1 tsp baking soda
- Pinch of salt
- 3/4 cup sugar
- 1 large egg, beaten
- 1 tsp vanilla extract
- 1 1/2 cups all-purpose flour

Instructions

1. Preheat oven to 350°F. Grease a loaf pan.
2. In a large bowl, mash the bananas with a fork. Stir in melted butter.
3. Mix in baking soda, salt, sugar, egg, and vanilla extract.
4. Add flour and stir until just combined.
5. Pour the batter into the prepared loaf pan and bake for 60-65 minutes, or until golden brown and a toothpick inserted comes out clean.
6. Let cool before slicing.

Grandma's Cabbage Rolls

Ingredients

- 1 medium cabbage
- 1 lb ground beef
- 1 cup cooked rice
- 1 onion, chopped
- 1 can (15 oz) tomato sauce
- 1 can (14.5 oz) diced tomatoes
- 1 tbsp brown sugar
- 1 tbsp lemon juice
- Salt and pepper to taste

Instructions

1. Preheat oven to 350°F. Grease a baking dish.
2. Bring a large pot of water to a boil. Cut the core from the cabbage and carefully peel off the leaves. Blanch the leaves in boiling water until soft, about 2 minutes.
3. In a bowl, combine ground beef, cooked rice, chopped onion, salt, and pepper.
4. Place about 1/4 cup of the beef mixture in the center of each cabbage leaf and roll up, tucking in the sides.
5. Arrange the cabbage rolls seam-side down in the baking dish.
6. In a separate bowl, mix together tomato sauce, diced tomatoes, brown sugar, and lemon juice. Pour over the cabbage rolls.

7. Cover with foil and bake for 1.5 hours, or until the rolls are tender.

Aunt June's Potato Salad

Ingredients

- 4 large potatoes, peeled and cubed
- 1/2 cup mayonnaise
- 2 tbsp Dijon mustard
- 1 tbsp apple cider vinegar
- 1/4 cup chopped celery
- 1/4 cup chopped onion
- 2 hard-boiled eggs, chopped
- Salt and pepper to taste

Instructions

1. Bring a pot of salted water to a boil. Add potatoes and cook until tender, about 10-15 minutes. Drain and let cool.
2. In a large bowl, mix together mayonnaise, Dijon mustard, and apple cider vinegar.
3. Add the cooled potatoes, celery, onion, and hard-boiled eggs. Stir gently to combine.
4. Season with salt and pepper to taste. Chill in the refrigerator for at least 1 hour before serving.

Dad's Barbecue Ribs

Ingredients

- 2 racks of baby back ribs
- 1/4 cup brown sugar
- 1/4 cup paprika
- 1 tbsp garlic powder
- 1 tbsp onion powder
- 1 tsp salt
- 1/2 tsp black pepper
- 1/2 tsp cayenne pepper
- 1 cup barbecue sauce

Instructions

1. Preheat oven to 275°F. Line a baking sheet with aluminum foil.
2. Remove the membrane from the ribs and place them on the prepared baking sheet.
3. In a small bowl, mix together brown sugar, paprika, garlic powder, onion powder, salt, pepper, and cayenne pepper.
4. Rub the spice mixture all over the ribs.
5. Cover the ribs with foil and bake for 2.5-3 hours, or until tender.
6. Preheat a grill or grill pan to medium-high heat. Brush the ribs with barbecue sauce and grill for 5-10 minutes, basting with more sauce, until caramelized and

slightly crispy.

7. Serve hot with extra barbecue sauce on the side.

Mom's Chicken and Dumplings

Ingredients

- 4 chicken breasts or thighs, boneless and skinless
- 4 cups chicken broth
- 1 onion, chopped
- 2 carrots, sliced
- 2 celery stalks, chopped
- 3 cloves garlic, minced
- 2 cups all-purpose flour
- 1/2 cup milk
- 1/4 cup butter
- 1 tsp baking powder
- 1/2 tsp salt
- 1/4 tsp pepper
- 2 tsp fresh parsley, chopped

Instructions

1. In a large pot, bring chicken broth to a boil. Add chicken breasts, onion, carrots, celery, and garlic. Simmer for 20-25 minutes, or until chicken is cooked through.

2. Remove chicken from the pot and shred using two forks. Return chicken to the pot.

3. In a bowl, mix flour, milk, butter, baking powder, salt, and pepper to form a dough. Drop spoonfuls of dough into the simmering soup. Cover and cook for 10-12 minutes, or until dumplings are cooked through.

4. Garnish with fresh parsley and serve hot.

Great-Grandmother's Frittata

Ingredients

- 8 large eggs
- 1/2 cup heavy cream
- 1 cup diced potatoes, cooked
- 1/2 cup diced onion
- 1/2 cup diced bell pepper
- 1 cup shredded cheese (cheddar, mozzarella, or a blend)
- 1/2 cup cooked bacon or sausage, crumbled
- Salt and pepper to taste
- Fresh herbs for garnish (optional)

Instructions

1. Preheat the oven to 375°F. Grease a 9-inch ovenproof skillet.
2. In a bowl, whisk together eggs, heavy cream, salt, and pepper.
3. In the prepared skillet, sauté onions and bell peppers until softened, about 5 minutes.
4. Add cooked potatoes and meat to the skillet, stirring to combine.
5. Pour the egg mixture over the ingredients in the skillet. Sprinkle with shredded cheese.
6. Bake for 20-25 minutes, or until the eggs are set and the top is golden brown.

7. Garnish with fresh herbs if desired and serve warm.

Grandma's Cinnamon Rolls

Ingredients

- 3 cups all-purpose flour
- 1/4 cup granulated sugar
- 1 packet active dry yeast (2 1/4 tsp)
- 1/2 cup warm milk
- 1/4 cup melted butter
- 1/2 tsp salt
- 2 large eggs
- 1/4 cup brown sugar
- 2 tbsp ground cinnamon
- 1/4 cup unsalted butter, softened
- 1 cup powdered sugar
- 2 tbsp milk
- 1 tsp vanilla extract

Instructions

1. In a bowl, combine warm milk and sugar. Stir in yeast and let it sit for 5-10 minutes until frothy.
2. Add melted butter, salt, and eggs to the yeast mixture. Gradually stir in flour until a dough forms.

3. Knead the dough for 5-7 minutes until smooth. Cover and let rise in a warm place for 1-2 hours.

4. Preheat oven to 350°F and grease a baking dish.

5. Roll out dough on a floured surface to 1/4-inch thickness. Spread softened butter over the dough, then sprinkle with brown sugar and cinnamon.

6. Roll the dough up tightly and cut into 12 slices. Place the slices in the prepared baking dish and bake for 20-25 minutes, until golden brown.

7. While the rolls bake, mix powdered sugar, milk, and vanilla to make the glaze.

8. Drizzle the glaze over warm rolls and serve.

Family Roast Beef with Gravy

Ingredients

- 3-4 lb beef roast (sirloin or chuck)
- 1 tbsp olive oil
- 1 tbsp salt
- 1 tsp black pepper
- 1 tbsp garlic powder
- 1 tbsp onion powder
- 2 cups beef broth
- 1 tbsp flour (for thickening)
- 1/4 cup red wine (optional)

Instructions

1. Preheat oven to 350°F. Rub beef roast with olive oil, salt, pepper, garlic powder, and onion powder.
2. Place the roast on a rack in a roasting pan. Roast for 1.5 to 2 hours, or until the internal temperature reaches 135°F for medium-rare.
3. Remove the roast from the oven and let it rest for 10-15 minutes before slicing.
4. For the gravy, place the roasting pan on the stovetop over medium heat. Add beef broth and red wine (if using), scraping up any browned bits from the pan.
5. Whisk in flour and simmer for 5-7 minutes until the gravy thickens. Serve with sliced roast beef.

Aunt Millie's Creamy Coleslaw

Ingredients

- 4 cups shredded cabbage
- 1/2 cup shredded carrots
- 1/4 cup chopped onion
- 1/2 cup mayonnaise
- 2 tbsp apple cider vinegar
- 1 tbsp honey
- 1 tsp Dijon mustard
- Salt and pepper to taste

Instructions

1. In a large bowl, combine shredded cabbage, carrots, and onion.
2. In a separate bowl, whisk together mayonnaise, vinegar, honey, mustard, salt, and pepper.
3. Pour the dressing over the cabbage mixture and toss to coat evenly.
4. Cover and refrigerate for at least 1 hour before serving.

Mom's Tomato Soup

Ingredients

- 1 can (28 oz) crushed tomatoes
- 1 cup chicken or vegetable broth
- 1/2 cup heavy cream
- 1/2 onion, chopped
- 2 cloves garlic, minced
- 1 tbsp olive oil
- Salt and pepper to taste
- Fresh basil for garnish

Instructions

1. In a large pot, heat olive oil over medium heat. Add onions and garlic and sauté until softened, about 5 minutes.
2. Add crushed tomatoes and broth, bringing the mixture to a simmer.
3. Let the soup cook for 15-20 minutes, stirring occasionally.
4. Stir in heavy cream and season with salt and pepper to taste.
5. Use an immersion blender to blend the soup until smooth (or transfer to a blender in batches).
6. Serve with fresh basil and crusty bread.

Grandma's Peach Cobbler

Ingredients

- 4 cups fresh or frozen peaches, sliced
- 1 cup granulated sugar
- 1 tbsp lemon juice
- 1/4 tsp cinnamon
- 1 1/2 cups all-purpose flour
- 2 tsp baking powder
- 1/2 tsp salt
- 1/2 cup unsalted butter, melted
- 1 cup milk
- 1/2 tsp vanilla extract

Instructions

1. Preheat oven to 350°F and grease a 9-inch baking dish.
2. In a bowl, combine peaches, sugar, lemon juice, and cinnamon. Pour the mixture into the prepared baking dish.
3. In a separate bowl, mix flour, baking powder, and salt. Add melted butter, milk, and vanilla extract. Stir until just combined.
4. Spoon the batter over the peaches, covering them as best as you can.
5. Bake for 40-45 minutes, until golden brown and bubbly.

6. Let cool slightly before serving with vanilla ice cream.

Dad's Fried Chicken

Ingredients

- 4 chicken breasts or thighs, bone-in, skin-on
- 2 cups buttermilk
- 1 tbsp hot sauce
- 2 cups all-purpose flour
- 1 tbsp garlic powder
- 1 tbsp onion powder
- 1 tsp paprika
- Salt and pepper to taste
- Vegetable oil for frying

Instructions

1. In a large bowl, combine buttermilk and hot sauce. Add chicken pieces, cover, and refrigerate for at least 2 hours or overnight.
2. In another bowl, mix flour, garlic powder, onion powder, paprika, salt, and pepper.
3. Heat oil in a deep skillet or fryer to 350°F.
4. Dredge each piece of chicken in the flour mixture, pressing down lightly to coat evenly.
5. Fry the chicken in batches, cooking for 10-12 minutes per side, or until golden brown and cooked through.
6. Drain on paper towels and serve hot.

Nana's Homemade Jam

Ingredients

- 4 cups fresh fruit (strawberries, peaches, or mixed berries)
- 2 cups granulated sugar
- 1 tbsp lemon juice
- 1/4 tsp cinnamon (optional)
- 1 packet pectin (optional)

Instructions

1. In a large pot, combine fruit, sugar, and lemon juice. Cook over medium heat until the fruit breaks down and the mixture thickens, about 30-40 minutes.
2. If using, stir in pectin and cook for an additional 5-10 minutes.
3. Pour the jam into sterilized jars and seal. Let cool to room temperature before refrigerating.
4. Store in the fridge for up to 2 weeks or process in a water bath for longer storage.

Great-Aunt's Stuffing Recipe

Ingredients

- 1 loaf of day-old bread, cubed
- 1 cup celery, chopped
- 1/2 cup onion, chopped
- 1/2 cup unsalted butter
- 2 cups chicken or vegetable broth
- 1 tsp sage
- 1 tsp thyme
- 1/2 tsp rosemary
- Salt and pepper to taste
- 1/2 cup fresh parsley, chopped

Instructions

1. Preheat oven to 350°F and grease a baking dish.
2. In a skillet, melt butter over medium heat. Add celery and onion and cook until softened, about 5 minutes.
3. Add the bread cubes to the skillet and toss to combine with the vegetables.
4. Pour in the chicken or vegetable broth and stir until the bread has absorbed the liquid. Season with sage, thyme, rosemary, salt, and pepper.
5. Transfer the stuffing to the prepared baking dish and cover with foil.

6. Bake for 25-30 minutes. Remove foil and bake for an additional 10 minutes to crisp the top.

7. Garnish with fresh parsley and serve.

Family Beef Tacos

Ingredients

- 1 lb ground beef
- 1/2 onion, chopped
- 1 packet taco seasoning
- 1/4 cup water
- 8 soft or hard taco shells
- Toppings: shredded lettuce, diced tomatoes, shredded cheese, sour cream, salsa, guacamole, cilantro, lime wedges

Instructions

1. In a skillet, cook ground beef and onion over medium heat until browned, about 5-7 minutes. Drain excess fat.
2. Add taco seasoning and water to the beef, stirring to combine. Simmer for 5-10 minutes, or until the sauce thickens.
3. Heat taco shells according to package instructions.
4. Spoon the beef mixture into taco shells and add your favorite toppings.
5. Serve with lime wedges and extra salsa.

Great-Grandmother's Chicken Noodle Soup

Ingredients

- 4 chicken breasts or thighs, boneless and skinless
- 6 cups chicken broth
- 2 carrots, sliced
- 2 celery stalks, chopped
- 1 onion, chopped
- 2 cloves garlic, minced
- 1 tsp dried thyme
- 1 bay leaf
- 2 cups egg noodles
- Salt and pepper to taste
- Fresh parsley, chopped (for garnish)

Instructions

1. In a large pot, combine chicken, chicken broth, carrots, celery, onion, garlic, thyme, and bay leaf.
2. Bring to a boil, then reduce heat and simmer for 20-25 minutes, or until chicken is fully cooked.
3. Remove the chicken from the pot, shred it using two forks, and return it to the soup.
4. Add the egg noodles and cook until tender, about 8-10 minutes.

5. Season with salt and pepper to taste. Garnish with fresh parsley and serve.

Mom's Stuffed Bell Peppers

Ingredients

- 4 large bell peppers, tops cut off and seeds removed
- 1 lb ground beef
- 1/2 cup onion, chopped
- 1 cup cooked rice
- 1 can (14.5 oz) diced tomatoes
- 1 tsp garlic powder
- 1 tsp dried basil
- 1 tsp dried oregano
- 1/2 cup shredded cheese (optional)
- Salt and pepper to taste

Instructions

1. Preheat oven to 375°F. Grease a baking dish.
2. In a skillet, cook ground beef and onion over medium heat until browned. Drain any excess fat.
3. Stir in cooked rice, diced tomatoes, garlic powder, basil, oregano, salt, and pepper. Simmer for 5 minutes to combine flavors.
4. Stuff the bell peppers with the beef mixture and place them in the prepared baking dish.

5. Cover with foil and bake for 25-30 minutes. If desired, sprinkle with cheese and bake for an additional 5-10 minutes until the cheese is melted and bubbly.

6. Serve hot.

Aunt Mary's Lemon Bars

Ingredients

- **For the crust:**
    - 1 1/2 cups all-purpose flour
    - 1/2 cup powdered sugar
    - 1/2 cup unsalted butter, softened
- **For the filling:**
    - 3 large eggs
    - 1 cup granulated sugar
    - 1/4 cup all-purpose flour
    - 1/4 cup freshly squeezed lemon juice
    - 1/4 tsp baking powder
    - Powdered sugar for dusting

Instructions

1. Preheat oven to 350°F. Grease and flour an 8x8-inch baking dish.
2. **Make the crust:** In a bowl, mix flour, powdered sugar, and butter until a dough forms. Press the dough evenly into the bottom of the prepared dish.
3. Bake the crust for 15-20 minutes, or until lightly golden.
4. **Make the filling:** In a separate bowl, whisk eggs, sugar, flour, lemon juice, and baking powder until smooth.

5. Pour the lemon mixture over the baked crust and return to the oven. Bake for 25-30 minutes, or until the filling is set and slightly golden.

6. Let cool completely before cutting into squares. Dust with powdered sugar before serving.

Grandma's Shrimp and Grits

Ingredients

- 1 lb shrimp, peeled and deveined
- 1 cup grits
- 4 cups chicken broth
- 2 tbsp unsalted butter
- 1/2 cup heavy cream
- 1 tsp garlic powder
- 1 tsp paprika
- 1/2 tsp cayenne pepper (optional)
- 1 tbsp lemon juice
- 1/2 cup chopped green onions
- Salt and pepper to taste

Instructions

1. In a large pot, bring chicken broth to a boil. Stir in the grits and reduce the heat. Simmer, stirring occasionally, for 20-25 minutes until thickened.

2. Stir in butter, heavy cream, garlic powder, paprika, cayenne pepper (if using), salt, and pepper. Keep warm.

3. In a skillet, sauté shrimp in a little olive oil over medium heat until pink and cooked through, about 4-5 minutes. Add lemon juice and green onions.

4. Serve the shrimp over the creamy grits and garnish with additional green onions.

Family-Style Lasagna

Ingredients

- 1 lb ground beef
- 1 onion, chopped
- 2 cloves garlic, minced
- 1 can (28 oz) crushed tomatoes
- 1 can (6 oz) tomato paste
- 1 tsp dried basil
- 1 tsp dried oregano
- 1/2 tsp salt
- 1/4 tsp black pepper
- 12 lasagna noodles, cooked and drained
- 15 oz ricotta cheese
- 2 cups shredded mozzarella cheese
- 1/2 cup grated Parmesan cheese

Instructions

1. Preheat oven to 375°F. Grease a 9x13-inch baking dish.
2. In a skillet, cook ground beef, onion, and garlic until browned. Drain excess fat.
3. Stir in crushed tomatoes, tomato paste, basil, oregano, salt, and pepper. Simmer for 20 minutes.

4. In the prepared baking dish, layer cooked lasagna noodles, ricotta cheese, meat sauce, and shredded mozzarella. Repeat layers, finishing with meat sauce on top. Sprinkle with Parmesan cheese.

5. Cover with foil and bake for 30-35 minutes. Remove foil and bake for an additional 10 minutes until bubbly and golden.

6. Let cool for 10 minutes before slicing and serving.

Dad's Clam Chowder

Ingredients

- 2 cans (6.5 oz each) clam meat, drained
- 2 cups chicken broth
- 2 cups heavy cream
- 1/2 cup celery, chopped
- 1/2 cup onion, chopped
- 2 medium potatoes, peeled and diced
- 1/4 cup unsalted butter
- 1 tsp garlic powder
- 1/2 tsp thyme
- Salt and pepper to taste

Instructions

1. In a large pot, melt butter over medium heat. Add celery, onion, and potatoes and sauté until softened, about 5-7 minutes.
2. Add chicken broth, heavy cream, garlic powder, thyme, salt, and pepper. Bring to a simmer and cook for 15-20 minutes, or until potatoes are tender.
3. Stir in the clam meat and cook for an additional 5 minutes to heat through.
4. Serve hot with crusty bread.

Grandma's Rhubarb Pie

Ingredients

- 4 cups rhubarb, chopped
- 1 1/2 cups granulated sugar
- 1/4 cup all-purpose flour
- 1/4 tsp cinnamon
- 1 tbsp lemon juice
- 2 tbsp butter
- 1 package pie crust (2 crusts)

Instructions

1. Preheat oven to 425°F. Line a 9-inch pie dish with one pie crust.
2. In a bowl, combine rhubarb, sugar, flour, cinnamon, and lemon juice. Stir to combine.
3. Pour the mixture into the prepared pie crust. Dot with butter and cover with the second pie crust. Crimp the edges to seal.
4. Cut a few slits in the top crust to allow steam to escape.
5. Bake for 40-45 minutes, or until the crust is golden and the filling is bubbling.
6. Let cool before serving.

Aunt Betty's Pecan Pie

Ingredients

- 1 1/2 cups pecan halves
- 3/4 cup light corn syrup
- 3/4 cup granulated sugar
- 1/4 cup unsalted butter, melted
- 3 large eggs
- 1 tsp vanilla extract
- 1/4 tsp salt
- 1 pie crust (store-bought or homemade)

Instructions

1. Preheat oven to 350°F. Line a 9-inch pie dish with pie crust.
2. In a bowl, whisk together corn syrup, sugar, melted butter, eggs, vanilla extract, and salt.
3. Stir in pecans and pour the mixture into the pie crust.
4. Bake for 45-50 minutes, or until the pie is set and the crust is golden.
5. Let cool completely before serving.

Mom's Baked Ziti

Ingredients

- 1 lb ziti pasta
- 1 lb ground beef or Italian sausage
- 1 jar (24 oz) marinara sauce
- 1 can (14.5 oz) crushed tomatoes
- 2 cups ricotta cheese
- 2 cups shredded mozzarella cheese
- 1/2 cup grated Parmesan cheese
- 1 egg
- 2 cloves garlic, minced
- 1 tsp dried oregano
- Salt and pepper to taste
- Fresh basil for garnish (optional)

Instructions

1. Preheat oven to 375°F. Cook the ziti pasta according to package instructions, then drain and set aside.

2. In a skillet, cook ground beef or sausage over medium heat until browned. Drain excess fat, then add garlic and cook for an additional minute.

3. Stir in marinara sauce, crushed tomatoes, oregano, salt, and pepper. Simmer for 10-15 minutes.

4. In a bowl, mix ricotta cheese, 1 cup mozzarella, Parmesan cheese, and egg. Stir until combined.

5. In a large baking dish, layer cooked pasta, meat sauce, and cheese mixture, repeating layers. Top with the remaining mozzarella cheese.

6. Bake for 25-30 minutes, until bubbly and golden. Garnish with fresh basil if desired.

Great-Grandmother's Goulash

Ingredients

- 1 lb ground beef
- 1 onion, chopped
- 1 green bell pepper, chopped
- 2 cloves garlic, minced
- 1 can (14.5 oz) diced tomatoes
- 1 can (6 oz) tomato paste
- 1 cup beef broth
- 2 tsp paprika
- 1 tsp dried oregano
- 1/2 tsp dried basil
- Salt and pepper to taste
- 2 cups elbow macaroni, cooked and drained
- 1/2 cup shredded cheddar cheese (optional)

Instructions

1. In a large skillet, cook ground beef, onion, and bell pepper over medium heat until browned. Drain excess fat, then add garlic and cook for an additional minute.

2. Stir in diced tomatoes, tomato paste, beef broth, paprika, oregano, basil, salt, and pepper. Bring to a simmer and cook for 15-20 minutes.

3. Stir in the cooked elbow macaroni and mix until well combined.

4. Serve with shredded cheddar cheese on top, if desired.

Nana's Chicken Fried Steak

Ingredients

- 4 beef cube steaks
- 1 cup all-purpose flour
- 1 tsp garlic powder
- 1 tsp onion powder
- 1 tsp paprika
- Salt and pepper to taste
- 2 large eggs, beaten
- 1 cup buttermilk
- 1 cup vegetable oil for frying

Instructions

1. In a shallow dish, combine flour, garlic powder, onion powder, paprika, salt, and pepper.
2. Dip each cube steak into the beaten eggs, then coat with the seasoned flour mixture.
3. In a large skillet, heat vegetable oil over medium heat. Fry the steaks for 4-5 minutes on each side, until golden brown and crispy.
4. Remove the steaks from the skillet and drain on paper towels.
5. Serve with mashed potatoes and gravy, if desired.

Family Meatloaf Sandwiches

Ingredients

- 1 lb ground beef
- 1/2 cup breadcrumbs
- 1/4 cup milk
- 1 egg
- 1/2 cup onion, chopped
- 1/4 cup ketchup
- 1 tsp Worcestershire sauce
- Salt and pepper to taste
- 4 sandwich buns
- Lettuce, tomato, and cheese for toppings

Instructions

1. Preheat oven to 350°F. In a large bowl, combine ground beef, breadcrumbs, milk, egg, onion, ketchup, Worcestershire sauce, salt, and pepper.
2. Shape the mixture into a loaf and place it on a baking sheet.
3. Bake for 45-50 minutes, or until cooked through.
4. Let the meatloaf rest for 10 minutes before slicing.
5. Serve the meatloaf on sandwich buns with your choice of toppings, such as lettuce, tomato, and cheese.

Great-Aunt's Green Bean Casserole

Ingredients

- 2 cups fresh green beans, trimmed
- 1 can (10.5 oz) cream of mushroom soup
- 1/2 cup milk
- 1 cup French fried onions
- 1 cup shredded cheddar cheese
- Salt and pepper to taste

Instructions

1. Preheat oven to 350°F. Cook the green beans in boiling water for 3-4 minutes, then drain.

2. In a large bowl, combine cream of mushroom soup, milk, salt, and pepper. Add the cooked green beans and mix to combine.

3. Transfer the mixture to a greased baking dish. Top with French fried onions and shredded cheddar cheese.

4. Bake for 20-25 minutes, until bubbly and golden. Serve hot.

Mom's Chocolate Pudding Cake

Ingredients

- 1 cup all-purpose flour
- 3/4 cup granulated sugar
- 1/2 tsp baking powder
- 1/4 tsp salt
- 2 tbsp unsweetened cocoa powder
- 1/2 cup milk
- 1/4 cup unsalted butter, melted
- 1 tsp vanilla extract
- 1/2 cup brown sugar
- 1 cup hot water

Instructions

1. Preheat oven to 350°F. Grease a 9x9-inch baking dish.
2. In a bowl, mix flour, sugar, baking powder, salt, and cocoa powder. Stir in milk, butter, and vanilla extract until combined.
3. Pour the batter into the prepared baking dish.
4. In a separate bowl, mix brown sugar and hot water. Pour the mixture over the batter (do not stir).
5. Bake for 35-40 minutes, until the cake is set and the pudding is bubbly. Serve warm with whipped cream or vanilla ice cream.

Grandma's Steamed Pudding

Ingredients

- 1 cup all-purpose flour
- 1/2 cup brown sugar
- 1/2 cup butter, softened
- 1/2 cup milk
- 1 large egg
- 1 tsp baking powder
- 1 tsp ground cinnamon
- 1/2 tsp ground nutmeg
- 1/4 tsp salt
- 1/2 cup raisins or currants (optional)
- 1/4 cup maple syrup

Instructions

1. Grease a 1.5-quart pudding basin or heatproof bowl.
2. In a large bowl, cream the butter and brown sugar until light and fluffy.
3. Add the egg and mix well. Stir in the milk.
4. In a separate bowl, whisk together the flour, baking powder, cinnamon, nutmeg, and salt. Gradually fold the dry ingredients into the wet ingredients.
5. Stir in raisins or currants, if using.

6. Pour the batter into the prepared pudding basin and cover tightly with foil or parchment paper.

7. Place the pudding basin in a large pot of boiling water (about halfway up the sides of the bowl) and steam for 1.5-2 hours, checking occasionally to ensure there is enough water in the pot.

8. Once done, remove from the pot and allow to cool for 5-10 minutes before serving.

9. Drizzle with maple syrup and enjoy!

Dad's Smoked Sausages

Ingredients

- 4 pork sausages (or your preferred sausage type)
- 1/4 cup apple cider vinegar
- 1/4 cup water
- 1 tbsp smoked paprika
- 1 tsp garlic powder
- 1 tsp onion powder
- 1 tsp brown sugar
- Salt and pepper to taste
- Wood chips for smoking (hickory or applewood preferred)

Instructions

1. Preheat your smoker to 225°F.
2. In a small bowl, mix the apple cider vinegar, water, smoked paprika, garlic powder, onion powder, brown sugar, salt, and pepper.
3. Brush the sausages with the vinegar and spice mixture, coating evenly.
4. Place the sausages in the smoker and smoke for 1.5-2 hours, turning occasionally, until they reach an internal temperature of 160°F.
5. Remove from the smoker and let rest for a few minutes before serving.

Aunt Diane's Potato Soup

Ingredients

- 4 large russet potatoes, peeled and diced
- 1 small onion, chopped
- 2 cloves garlic, minced
- 4 cups chicken broth
- 1 cup heavy cream
- 1/2 cup shredded cheddar cheese
- 1/4 cup chopped green onions
- Salt and pepper to taste
- 4 slices cooked bacon, crumbled (optional)

Instructions

1. In a large pot, sauté the onion and garlic in a bit of butter or oil over medium heat for 3-4 minutes until soft.
2. Add the diced potatoes and chicken broth. Bring to a boil, then reduce heat to a simmer. Cook until the potatoes are tender, about 15-20 minutes.
3. Use an immersion blender to partially blend the soup, leaving some chunks for texture, or transfer half the soup to a blender and blend until smooth before returning it to the pot.
4. Stir in the heavy cream and cheddar cheese, and cook until the cheese is melted and the soup is creamy.
5. Season with salt and pepper to taste.

6. Serve hot, garnished with green onions and crumbled bacon if desired.

Nana's Chocolate Fudge

Ingredients

- 2 cups semisweet chocolate chips
- 1 can (14 oz) sweetened condensed milk
- 1/4 cup unsalted butter
- 1 tsp vanilla extract
- Pinch of salt

Instructions

1. Line an 8x8-inch baking dish with parchment paper or aluminum foil.
2. In a saucepan over low heat, melt the chocolate chips, sweetened condensed milk, and butter, stirring frequently until smooth.
3. Remove from heat and stir in the vanilla extract and a pinch of salt.
4. Pour the fudge mixture into the prepared baking dish and spread evenly.
5. Refrigerate for at least 2 hours until firm. Cut into squares and serve.

Great-Grandmother's Rice Pudding

Ingredients

- 1 cup cooked white rice
- 2 cups whole milk
- 1/2 cup heavy cream
- 1/2 cup granulated sugar
- 1/2 tsp ground cinnamon
- 1/4 tsp salt
- 1 tsp vanilla extract
- 1/4 cup raisins (optional)

Instructions

1. In a medium saucepan, combine the cooked rice, milk, heavy cream, sugar, cinnamon, and salt. Bring to a simmer over medium heat, stirring occasionally.
2. Cook for 20-25 minutes, stirring frequently, until the mixture thickens and the rice is tender.
3. Stir in the vanilla extract and raisins (if using).
4. Remove from heat and let cool for 5 minutes before serving. Serve warm or chilled.

Mom's Apple Crisp

Ingredients

- 6 medium apples, peeled, cored, and sliced
- 1 tbsp lemon juice
- 1/2 cup granulated sugar
- 1/2 tsp ground cinnamon
- 1/4 tsp ground nutmeg
- 1/2 cup rolled oats
- 1/2 cup all-purpose flour
- 1/4 cup brown sugar
- 1/4 cup unsalted butter, cubed
- Pinch of salt

Instructions

1. Preheat oven to 350°F. Grease a 9x9-inch baking dish.
2. In a large bowl, toss the sliced apples with lemon juice, granulated sugar, cinnamon, and nutmeg. Transfer the apple mixture to the prepared baking dish.
3. In a separate bowl, mix the oats, flour, brown sugar, butter, and salt until the mixture forms a crumbly topping.
4. Sprinkle the topping evenly over the apples.
5. Bake for 40-45 minutes, until the apples are tender and the topping is golden brown.

6. Serve warm with a scoop of vanilla ice cream or whipped cream.

www.ingramcontent.com/pod-product-compliance
Lightning Source LLC
LaVergne TN
LVHW081618060526
838201LV00054B/2299